FIND YOUR WAY DISCUSSION GUIDE

FIND *your* WAY

DISCUSSION GUIDE

A Three-Session Guide to
Unleashing Your Greatest Potential

CARLY FIORINA
WITH ASHLEY WIERSMA

TYNDALE
MOMENTUM®

*The nonfiction imprint of
Tyndale House Publishers, Inc.*

Visit Tyndale online at www.tyndale.com.

Visit Tyndale Momentum online at www.tyndalemomentum.com.

TYNDALE, *Tyndale Momentum*, and Tyndale's quill logo are registered trademarks of Tyndale House Publishers, Inc. The Tyndale Momentum logo is a trademark of Tyndale House Publishers, Inc. Tyndale Momentum is the nonfiction imprint of Tyndale House Publishers, Inc., Carol Stream, Illinois.

The Leadership Framework is a registered trademark of Carly Fiorina.

Find Your Way Discussion Guide: A Three-Session Guide to Unleashing Your Greatest Potential

Published in association with the literary agency of AGI Vigliano Literary LLC, 16 East 77th Street, 3rd Floor, New York, NY 10075.

For information about special discounts for bulk purchases, please contact Tyndale House Publishers at csresponse@tyndale.com, or call 1-800-323-9400.

ISBN 978-1-4964-3576-7

Printed in the United States of America

25 24 23 22 21 20 19
7 6 5 4 3 2 1

CONTENTS

A NOTE FROM CARLY

I WAS A HAPPY, ACTIVE CHILD, but I was also filled with fear. Vivid dreams haunted many of my nights, and sometimes I was certain I saw visions—usually frightening ones. At a young age, I became aware that my mother's mother and my father's father had died when my parents were ten and thirteen, respectively. Intuitively, I understood what a tragedy this was and how it continued to deeply affect my mother and father. As I absorbed this part of my family's history, my greatest fear, whenever I was separated from them, became that my parents would die unexpectedly, or that I would die.

Perhaps because I was so afraid, Jesus became a constant, reassuring presence in my life. I loved the Bible stories we read together as a family or that I heard in Sunday school, and whenever I felt that familiar dread creep in at night, I would recite the Lord's Prayer, over and over again. Whenever my parents went out for the evening, I would pray in the same way. And still, to this day, the Lord's Prayer anchors my most fervent prayers.

As I grew older and established myself in the corporate

world, my faith remained, though it became something of an abstraction. I still prayed every day. I still knew that we reap what we sow. I still believed that "this life" is not the end. But I tended to see God as something of a super CEO, a leader of a massive enterprise, someone who had created the universe and catalyzed a sophisticated set of management processes that kept things running—not necessarily smoothly—over the long arc of time. He didn't attend to every detail, and he didn't know every person . . . how could he possibly? But he did receive regular management reports that directed his attention to strategic issues requiring intervention. Jesus Christ, the Holy Spirit, the Resurrection—these were profound ideas at the heart of a complex governance system, but I wasn't sure anymore that they were real.

Years went by. As fate's wicked humor would have it, I faced the heartbreak of my mother's unexpected death. When I received word that her health was failing rapidly, I was far away from her and unable to reach her side before she had lost her ability to communicate. Without a personal connection with Jesus at the time, I felt as if my heart might never heal. Later, when I took on huge challenges as CEO of Hewlett-Packard and felt immense loneliness in the process, I missed the spiritual intimacy I saw in others' lives. I wanted a refresher course for my faith.

During that season of seeking, I prayed for guidance and asked for signs. And on Christmas morning in 2007, I awoke with a crystal clear mind. I realized that there were signs all around me, many of them from the world of science and technology. Were there not inexplicable mysteries that confronted us every day? Were the building blocks and the origins of the universe not plain to see? Did Einstein not prove that energy never dies but merely changes form? I thought about the GPS in my car and marveled at the human ingenuity that could devise a system of technologies that keeps precise track of where each of us is, and that knows when we deviate off course and provides precise instructions to return us to the right path. If human beings can do this, I thought, then certainly God knows everything that is happening in the universe—not in broad, management strokes, but in minute, personal detail. And because God knows all, and knows us all so well, his care was instantiated in a physical, empathetic Son . . . not because God needed him, but because *we* did.

A short time later, when my father died, I grieved deeply but felt none of the awful turmoil that had accompanied my mother's death. The following year, when I was diagnosed with breast cancer, I came to understand the depth of God's love in a time of terrible passages: I battled my way through eleven rounds of surgery, underwent four months of chemotherapy, and endured ten weeks of radiation. Yet, through it all, I felt a deep peace. I realized that, despite its many burdens, cancer had brought great blessings. This would have been a scandalous viewpoint for me to hold not many years before. The love of family, the nurture of friendship, the kindness of strangers, the joy of life—I came to appreciate all these things in new and profound ways. It was my battle with cancer that gave me the understanding that life is measured not in time, but in love, moments of grace, and positive contributions.

To my shock, my ordeal with cancer would seem swift

and easy by comparison to the battles faced by Frank's and my younger daughter, Lori. Soon after I finished my radiation treatments, Lori passed away, alone, in her apartment. The grief and guilt my husband and I felt were suffocating. Frank told me he had lost his faith: How could he believe that God loved him, if that same God could allow such a terrible thing to occur? I prayed that Frank would be given a sign somehow, and that his faith would be restored.

Just before Father's Day that year, Frank went out to the garage. A pile of boxes that had been hunkering in the corner for who knows how long caught his eye. For no particular reason, he decided to open one of them, and there, lying on top of other odds and ends, were four Father's Day cards from Lori. One of them contained a long letter that Lori had written to Frank years earlier, telling him what a fine father he was. Frank later told me that at the moment when he read "I love you" in Lori's own hand, he *knew* that Jesus loved him, and that Lori had found peace.

I've come to know that God indeed hears our prayers, and that he often answers them in ways that are very clear to us. That knowledge reknitted me to the faith of my youth and inspired me to grow by leaps and bounds from there, most notably in my love for God's Word.

I had always known that the Gospels were profound testaments of faith, but now I also saw them as powerful stories of true leadership. Everything I know about the potential within every one of us to change the order of things for the better and to lead well is reflected in the New Testament.

Leadership is never about position or title, as evidenced by history's greatest leader, Jesus, who possessed neither.

Leaders do not judge others by their circumstances; instead, they see possibilities in the people around them, just as Jesus saw potential in both the tax collector and the prostitute.

Leaders collaborate with others to achieve their goals, as evidenced by Jesus' decision to invite twelve societal outcasts, relative nobodies, to become his disciples and learn how to change the world.

Leaders aren't afraid to challenge the status quo. Indeed, they realize that changing things for the better requires challenging the way things are. Jesus was a disrupter who wasn't afraid to challenge the religious hierarchy or the elites of his day.

Leaders must take time for reflection, even as, fundamentally, they actively engage with the people and problems around them. Jesus' refusal to lead a merely contemplative life, to instead actively seek out and solve problems, is an example of this.

Finally, there is a good reason that the words of Scripture so often exhort us to be courageous: True leadership requires courage first and foremost—the courage to act and the courage to continue.

In my experience, people of true faith make better leaders than those who lack faith. Our faith teaches us *humility*; we learn that no one is inherently better than anyone else, and each of us is gifted by God. We learn *empathy* because we know that any one of us can fall, and all can be redeemed. We know that there are blessings to be had even in dark times, and so our realism about the difficulties we face is tempered by our *optimism* in the difference each of us can make. Humility, empathy, and optimism are essential components of true leadership—tenets we will discuss at length in the pages ahead.

It is my hope in this series that you will come to more deeply appreciate your own capacity for leadership; that you will more fully realize opportunities to collaborate with others, perhaps even those in your small group, to solve the problems that are in front of you; and that you and the people who share your burden will change the order of things for the better.

Faith is a choice.

Leadership is a choice.

My hope for you as you engage with this content is that you will keep making both of these choices, each and every day.

Carly Fiorina
Alexandria, Virginia

HOW TO USE THIS GUIDE

Welcome to this three-session, video-based curriculum, a companion guide to *Find Your Way: Unleash Your Power and Highest Potential.* We have put these three sessions together with you in mind, in hopes you will discover there are problems that *you* are meant to solve—not by pursuing some societally prescribed *plan*, but by following the unique *path* God has set before you and by maximizing the potential he has placed within you.

To get the most out of these three sessions, you will need the following:

- The three *Find Your Way* video sessions (available as the *Find Your Way DVD Curriculum* or through online streaming at www.rightnowmedia.org)
- A copy of the book *Find Your Way: Unleash Your Power and Highest Potential*
- Your favorite Bible (this guide looks to the New Living Translation, but any translation will work)
- A pen and extra paper or a journal, in case you need more space to log your thoughts

If you're not already part of a development-oriented small group through your church or organization, consider rallying a few friends, family members, or colleagues to walk through this experience together. Certainly, you can work through the content on your own, but the best growth happens in community. Though sharing your burdens aloud in the presence of others can feel a little scary at first, the support and strength you'll gain as a result of traveling the path with others will be worth it in the end.

Once you confirm who will be joining you for the journey, choose a time and date to kick things off, and decide how often you will meet. This guide is arranged in three sessions, but you can divide them across three lunches, three weekly meetings, or some other interval that works for your group.

Feel free to share or rotate leadership responsibilities; or you can designate one member as the point person for all three sessions. In each session, facilitation cues appear at the beginning of the following eight sections:

1. **Summary**: An overview of the theme(s) covered in the session.
2. **The Full Story**: Relevant reading for the session from *Find Your Way*.
3. **First Thoughts**: An opening icebreaker for group discussion.
4. **From *Find Your Way***: A key passage from the book that focuses your group's thoughts on the central themes of the session.
5. **Video Notes**: Space to capture memorable quotes or useful insights from the session's video segment.

6. **Up for Discussion**: Questions for your group to discuss and answer.
7. **Now Go (and Grow)**: Session-specific action steps for group members to implement on their own.
8. **Looking for More?**: Questions, exercises, and experiments for group members to complete between sessions.

By God's grace, we can *show up*, *stand up*, and *solve something meaningful* in the days ahead. Let the problem solving begin.

session 1

THE PURPOSE OF THE PATH

A Word on the Problems
You're Meant to Solve

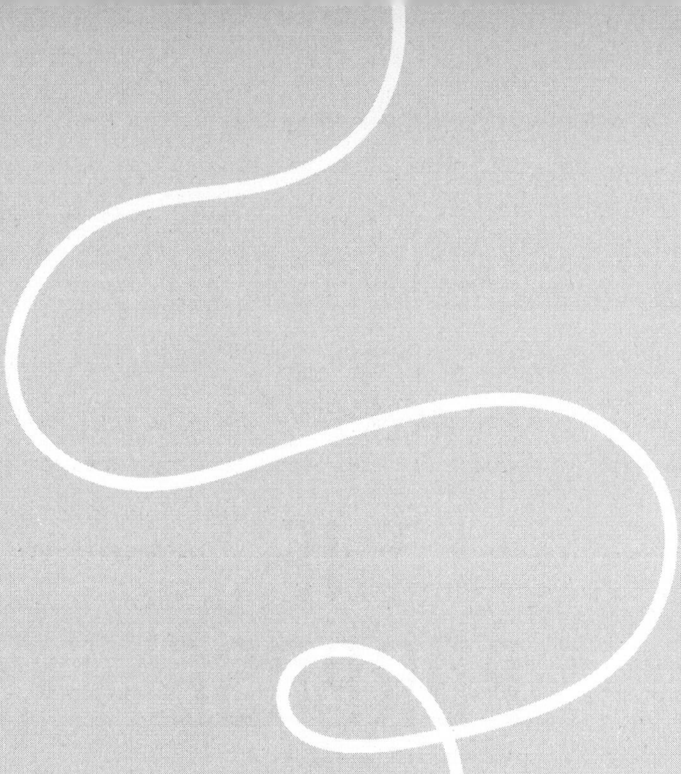

As you learn to harness the power within you, you will begin to make more sense out of life. You'll find that you really can patch up the brokenness of your past. You really can find purpose and meaning here and now. You really can make a positive impact on the world for decades to come.

Summary

We were created *on* purpose *for* a purpose, and that purpose is to solve meaningful problems that affect us and others in the world. But if this is true, why are we so quick to run *away* from problems—as if they're the enemy—rather than *toward* them, seeing problems as *opportunities*?

Session 1 exposes the lie that life is all about the *destination*—the eventual outcome, the society-approved plan. Instead, the key to fulfillment comes by following a *path* instead of a plan.

As you journey toward who you are meant to be, you will not always know where you're going. But knowing *who you are* and *whose you are* is all that matters in the end.

The Full Story

For more on the subjects covered in session 1, read the following chapters in *Find Your Way: Unleash Your Power and Highest Potential*:

- Moment of Revelation
- Chapter 1: Future You
- Chapter 2: The Tragedy of the Termite
- Chapter 3: What's Wrong Is Also What's Right

First Thoughts

As you settle in, have group members answer the following questions.

- When have you had your heart set on a specific outcome for your life and then were left disappointed in the end?

- In hindsight, are you grateful for how things turned out, or are you still disappointed deep inside?

From *Find Your Way*

To center your thoughts on this session's central topic, have a member of your group read the following excerpt aloud:

> It's natural to fall into a rut from time to time, where we wonder what we're doing, where we're going, and how it will all pan out in the end. Sometimes we know how we got there—a key relationship broke apart, a big push toward a goal came to an end, a milestone birthday showed up—and sometimes we have no clue how or why life seems to have ground to a halt. Either way, our instinct in these situations is to find a way out of that rut. Not knowing what else to do, . . . we snap our fingers and hatch a plan.
>
> "I know what will fix this," we say. "I'll just get a new job!"
>
> "I'll move to a new city!"
>
> "I'll start dating again!"
>
> "I just need a new challenge! A new adventure! A tighter set of abs."
>
> We focus on that "one thing"—whatever it is—convinced in our hearts and minds that *it* will get

us going again. But that one thing, though perhaps alluring, isn't magical. There is only so much that a new direction can accomplish. The dirty little secret of a "destination mind-set"—of living life *on plan*—is that it fails to deliver what it promises. Not just occasionally, but *every time.* Having a plan promises success and certainty, promotion and stability, status and *cash.* But as I've seen countless times firsthand, it delivers the very opposite. For those who adopt an *on-plan* approach to life, there are only three outcomes possible:

- You get there, but you can't sustain it.
- You get there, but it can't sustain you.
- You never get there at all.

Find Your Way, PAGES 29–30

Video Notes

Use the space below to log notes and insights from this session's video segment.

On being lifted up

Your gift to God

The only limitless asset around

The plan versus the path

How to find the path

The pitfalls of problem solving

Talking about problems versus solving them

Hope in New Delhi

Letting our light shine

The problems you're meant to solve

Up for Discussion

Cover as many of the following discussion questions as time and group interest allow.

Potential as Asset

1. *Given the season of life you're in, what insights from this session's video segment did you find most relevant or meaningful, and why?*

2. *"Human potential is the only limitless resource in the world." Do you agree? Disagree? Why?*

3. *What percentage of your own potential do you believe you've reached? How did you arrive at that number?*

Are you satisfied with that percentage? Why or why not?

The "On-Plan" Life and Your Potential

1. *In her opening story, Carly describes a time when she knew she had to quit something—in this case, law school—that she felt obligated to complete. When have you experienced the same sensation that you absolutely must walk away from something important that you were involved in? Describe to the group the circumstances—and the outcome you pursued.*

I know what it's like to try to live someone else's dream, to strive for someone else's goal, and to attempt to get where I'm going by following someone else's plan. I know what that soul-level dissatisfaction feels like. I know the drudgery. I know the disappointment. I know the pain.

CARLY FIORINA

2. *When have you suffered at the hands of a destination mind-set? What were the circumstances, and what happened as a result? Take a moment to jot down your thoughts, and then share your insights with the group.*

____

____

____

3. *What do you suppose happens to our potential when we stay locked into a destination mind-set for years or even decades?*

____

____

____

4. *What benefits might we discover by deciding to let go of other people's expectations for our lives and following a path we can be proud of instead?*

____

____

____

> The truth is, there never was a plan. What there was instead was a *path*. A path of hard work and commitment to excellence, no matter the circumstances. A path of running toward problems instead of away from them.
>
> CARLY FIORINA

The Role of Faith in Reaching Our Potential

1. *What do you make of the story about the woman in New Delhi whose family and friends told her to settle down, that the problems she saw weren't her problems to solve? When have you seen this dynamic play out in your own life? Give an example of a time when you were able to solve a problem that, at first blush, seemed way over your head, beyond your capacity, or above your pay grade.*

2. *Throughout Scripture, we see plenty of examples of Jesus asking his followers to lift their heads, raise their sights, and get into the game. By his attitudes and assumptions and actions, it's as if he's saying, "You! Yes, you. You're the one you've been waiting for. That problem you're staring at isn't going to solve itself!"*

   Read each of the following three scenes aloud, noting on the lines that follow the role that Jesus was asking his followers to play in accomplishing his work.

LAZARUS IS RAISED FROM THE DEAD

When Jesus arrived at Bethany, he was told that Lazarus had already been in his grave for four days. . . .

Jesus had stayed outside the village, at the place where Martha met him. When the people who were at the house consoling Mary saw her leave so hastily, they assumed she was going to Lazarus's grave to weep. So they followed her there. . . .

When Jesus saw her weeping and saw the other people wailing with her, a deep anger welled up within him, and he was deeply troubled. "Where have you put him?" he asked them. . . .

Jesus was still angry as he arrived at the tomb, a cave with a stone rolled across its entrance. "Roll the stone aside," Jesus told them. . . .

So they rolled the stone aside. Then Jesus looked up to heaven and said, "Father, thank you for hearing me. You always hear me, but I said it out loud for the sake of the all these people standing here, so that they will believe you sent me." Then Jesus shouted, "Lazarus, come out!" And the dead man came out, his hands and feet bound in graveclothes, his face wrapped in a headcloth. Jesus told them, "Unwrap him and let him go!"

JOHN 11:17, 30-31, 33-34, 38-39, 41-44

PEOPLE ARE HEALED

One day Jesus called together his twelve disciples and gave them power and authority to cast out all demons and to heal all diseases. Then he sent them out to tell everyone about the Kingdom of God and to heal the sick. "Take nothing for your journey," he instructed them. "Don't take a walking stick, a traveler's bag, food, money, or even a change of clothes. Wherever you go, stay in the same house until you leave town. And if a town refuses to welcome you, shake its dust from your feet as you leave to show that you have abandoned those people to their fate."

So they began their circuit of the villages, preaching the Good News and healing the sick.

LUKE 9:1-6

THE MASSES ARE FED

That evening the disciples came to [Jesus] and said, "This is a remote place, and it's already getting late. Send the crowds away so they can go to the villages and buy food for themselves."

But Jesus said, "That isn't necessary—you feed them."

"But we have only five loaves of bread and two fish!" they answered.

"Bring them here," he said. Then he told the people to sit down on the grass. Jesus took the five loaves and two fish, looked up toward heaven, and blessed them. Then, breaking the loaves into pieces, he gave the bread to the disciples, who distributed it to the people. They all ate as much as they wanted, and afterward, the disciples picked up twelve baskets of leftovers.

MATTHEW 14:15-20

3. *Think back on your spiritual journey thus far. When have you felt "tapped by God" to cooperate with a plan of his? Maybe you felt prompted to start a conversation with a stranger, or to meet a financial need anonymously, or to enfold in community a group that had been chronically marginalized. Describe to your group the dynamics that were in play and what you did in response.*

4. *Immediately following the feeding of the five thousand, we encounter an interesting scene. Matthew 14:22-33 says this:*

> Jesus insisted that his disciples get back into the boat and cross to the other side of the lake, while he sent the people home. After sending them home, he went up into the hills by himself to pray. Night fell while he was there alone.
>
> Meanwhile, the disciples were in trouble far away from land, for a strong wind had risen, and they were fighting heavy waves. About three o'clock in the morning Jesus came toward them, walking on the water. When the disciples saw him walking on the water, they were terrified. In their fear, they cried out, "It's a ghost!"
>
> But Jesus spoke to them at once. "Don't be afraid," he said. "Take courage. I am here!"
>
> Then Peter called to him, "Lord, if it's really you, tell me to come to you, walking on the water."
>
> "Yes, come," Jesus said.
>
> So Peter went over the side of the boat and walked on the water toward Jesus. But when he saw the strong wind and the waves, he was terrified and began to sink. "Save me, Lord!" he shouted.
>
> Jesus immediately reached out and grabbed him. "You have so little faith," Jesus said. "Why did you doubt me?"
>
> When they climbed back into the boat, the wind stopped. Then the disciples worshiped him. "You really are the son of God!" they exclaimed.

How was it possible for Jesus' disciples to witness the miraculous feeding of five thousand people, and then, mere hours later, experience such trepidation and doubt?

____

____

____

5. *What role does faith play in the way you approach problems in life? Select from the options below and discuss your insights with the group.*

    - *"I've never really thought about the intersection between my spiritual life and the practical problems I face."*
    - *"I notice that as problems intensify, I turn to my faith more often."*
    - *"I rely heavily on my faith as a source of strength and sustenance for solving the problems I face."*
    - *"Here's how I would say it: '________________________________ ____________.'"*

6. *What role do you want your faith to play in your problem-solving process?*

____

____

____

Why Problems Stay Unsolved

1. *The video segment identifies two types of people: (1) those who see a problem, talk about the problem, and set about finding a solution to the problem; and (2) those who see a problem and talk about the problem, but never help to solve the problem. Here are some typical responses:*

- *"I'm excellent at spotting problems. Sticking around until they're resolved? Not exactly my strong suit."*
- *"I've never been great at detecting problems, but once I'm made aware of an issue, I tend to jump in right away to help."*
- *"I mostly keep to myself. I wouldn't say I'm big on finding or solving problems that exist outside of my immediate world."*
- *"I live, eat, and breathe problems. I can't help but spot them. I can't help but rant about them. I can't help but rally support to go solve them."*

Which of these profiles best describes you? Select one and share your thoughts with the group about why you made the selection you did.

2. *The people who experience the most fulfillment are those who learn not only to spot problems, but also how to solve them. Consider the image of a spiral that can be seen as either moving upward or downward.*

- *Problem avoiders tend to spiral downward, suffering from a level of angst and frustration that only increases over*

time. They are inclined toward feelings of hopelessness and helplessness, anger and fear, cynicism and depression, and they believe that life is out to get them.

- *Problem solvers, on the other hand, trend toward an ever-expanding sense of optimism and self-possession, gratitude and effectiveness, spiritedness and anticipation, and ultimately hope and peace.*

Now, no reasonable person would knowingly opt for the downward spiral. So, what keeps us from willingly—not to mention joyously—moving toward problems instead of away from them? What explanations might you give for why you've retreated along the way?

Whether we're talking about an introvert in a sea of type A personalities, a thoroughbred trying to survive in a donkey-paced work environment, an imaginative dreamer tucked inside an accountant, a willing friend who finds herself friendless, a contributor who questions her ability to contribute, or a would-be success story needing assurance that she won't fail, nobody in their right mind stays locked up voluntarily. And yet this is exactly what I see countless people do each day, in every imaginable vocation, location, and walk of life, when they forfeit the freedom that can be theirs. To keep your potential locked up is to look at the offer of all-encompassing liberation and say, "Thanks, but I think I'll pass."

CARLY FIORINA

3. *We have identified four pitfalls that tend to play a role in our unwillingness, or inability, to run toward the problems we were made to solve. Fill in the right-hand column in the grid below, noting examples in your own life of casualties—perhaps including yourself—you've seen snared by each trap. Place a check mark beside the one you fall into most often.*

PITFALL	DESCRIPTION	HOW YOU'VE SEEN IT PLAY OUT
☐ **No. 1:** Presumption of Innocence	**Key Theme:** *Abdication* **Motto:** "Not my problem." Marked by a lack of engagement and the refusal to take responsibility. "Not my circus; not my monkeys." We *see* the problem. We *understand* the problem. We grasp the *effects* that the problem has caused. And yet we don't jump in to help solve the problem.	
☐ **No. 2:** Rush to Judgment	**Key Theme:** *Misidentification* **Motto:** "I've got *just* the solution for that." Marked by presumption and pride. We think we know how to solve a problem without taking the time to assess it from all angles to accurately identify the source rather than just the symptoms.	

PITFALL	DESCRIPTION	HOW YOU'VE SEEN IT PLAY OUT
☐ **No. 3:** Failure to Launch	**Key Theme:** *Procrastination* **Motto:** "I don't know where to start." Marked by endlessly kicking problems down the road, either because the solution is not immediately obvious, or because we lack the will to overcome inertia and get started.	
☐ **No. 4:** Scarcity Mentality	**Key Theme:** *Resignation* **Motto:** "This problem will never be resolved." Marked by self-defeating declarations of certain gloom and doom. We're well aware of the problem, and that we're probably best suited to help solve it. But we're convinced we'll never figure it out, nothing will ever change, life is always out to get us, and there's no use trying anymore.	

4. *Keeping in mind the pitfall that you most closely identified with on the chart above, share your thoughts on the following two questions with your group:*
   - *What benefit, encouragement, realization, or step of growth do you think you have missed each time you succumbed to that pitfall?*
   - *Who, or what, has been able to pull you out of the pit along the way?*

___

___

___

Problems as Blessings, Not Burdens

You may have noticed that problems have a way of festering, persisting, and getting worse. This is because solving problems requires *change*, and most people *despise* change. And yet it is only by solving problems that we develop a deeper capacity for being present, taking action, serving well, and reaching the potential we've been striving toward . . . which in turn gives us greater resources for solving even bigger problems.

It may be difficult to imagine yourself actually *welcoming* problems, but that is precisely where we're headed—learning to view problems not as burdens, but as the blessings they are. The first step to adopting this perspective is *belief*.

As you prepare to close your group discussion, take a look at the "Now Go (and Grow)" ideas following. Are your group members ready to take these steps?

Now Go (and Grow)

Before dismissing your gathering, ask each member of the group how he or she plans to implement the following action steps.

1. *Mind your mind. As you heard in this session's video segment, you were created on purpose for a purpose, and that purpose is to solve problems that God says matter to him. Living into this grand potential begins with choosing to believe.*

    - *Believe that you were created on purpose, by the living, loving God.*
    - *Believe that you were created for a purpose, that your life is no accident, and that every day counts.*
    - *Believe that your life's purpose is to make a meaningful contribution, and that you have everything you need to achieve this goal.*
    - *Believe that you will someday reach your fullest potential . . . that you'll know fulfillment . . . that you'll know peace.*

    What refinements might you make to your assumptions or your attitudes, between now and your next group meeting, to help you mind your mind?

    ____

    ____

    ____

2. *Mind your mouth. What you believe matters greatly; but equally important is what you say. Change is hard enough without allowing self-sabotaging comments to undermine your efforts. Between now and your next group meeting, be mindful of the things you say—both to yourself in your head, and aloud. Commit to curtailing all negative self-talk over the coming*

week, and take stock of how much more certain and sure-footed you feel.

3. *Mind your ways. The natural by-product of taking greater care with your thoughts and your words is that your actions will start to shift as well. For now, simply anticipate that powerful dynamic, which we'll address more thoroughly in session 2.*

> As you assess your present set of circumstances, what do you see? What do you hear? What problems are raising their hands in your life, hoping you'll choose them to solve? What thoughts are cluttering your mind, just waiting to get sorted out? What situations are making your life more difficult these days? Who seems bound and determined to give you heartburn lately?
>
> CARLY FIORINA

Looking for More?

To dive deeper into the concepts presented in session 1, complete the following section on your own, before your next group meeting.

If you were excited to find this section here, you and Carly may be kindred spirits. She, too, has been accused of overachieving, fixating on the quest for more knowledge, and relentlessly pursuing personal application when presented with new concepts.

In this "Looking for More?" section, you will dig deeper on an extended excerpt from *Find Your Way*, engage with a few evaluative and introspective exercises, and experiment with applying the core concepts to your life.

The Excerpt

In chapter 3 of *Find Your Way*, Carly introduces us to Jim, an engineer she worked with at AT&T, whose story illustrates her theory that the best way to get started on the path to our fullest potential is by finding a meaningful problem to solve.

> [Jim] was one of those guys who fly below the radar most of the time. Every day, he arrived at work at the same time, parked in the same slot, ate lunch by himself at his desk, and departed at closing time, without causing a single stir. People looked past Jim; he kind of blended in that way. Most people would have described him as steady but unremarkable, dependable but average.

Because I had only recently become Jim's boss, I didn't know much about engineering, and I didn't know much about Jim. So one day I sat down and asked him to tell me about his job and what he did. And I asked him if he saw any problems in his work each day.

Jim eyed me for a moment, as if weighing whether to divulge what was on his mind.

"Well," he began, "there is something I've been wondering about . . ."

Jim designed circuits, and every month AT&T got billed for those circuits.

"I've noticed," he said, "that the circuit manufacturer's bills never exactly reflect the designs I provide."

"Well, what do you think we ought to do about that?" I asked.

"I think we ought to check 'em," Jim said.

I asked Jim to start checking those invoices. I secured resources for him so he could check them more thoroughly and more regularly. And lo and behold, Jim was right; we were being mischarged—and not by a little. Correcting those billing errors saved AT&T $300 million the first year alone. . . .

Jim was aware of the problem. He assumed, having raised the issue previously with no response, that no one was interested in solving it. Status quo was the way it was. When I came in search of problems, the problem was brought to light, clarified, and worked on. And eventually the problem was solved.

Solving that problem—a *massive* win for our team—not only saved the company millions of dollars, but it also deepened Jim's organizational credibility with his superiors, garnered additional support and respect from his peers, broadened his appreciation for the complexities of how things worked outside of his direct role, and increased his sense of self-confidence. The solving of this one immediate problem prepared Jim to solve even *bigger* problems in days to come. Problems are what pave the path to our full potential. Solving problems is what enables us to thrive.

Find Your Way, PAGES 44–46

The Evaluation

In sessions 2 and 3, we will look more closely at the nuts and bolts of solving problems, but for now, as you work to pinpoint one or two problems you'd like to work on, consider how the stop-look-listen approach (see chapter 3 in *Find Your Way*) was illustrated in this scenario.

STOP

How would you put into words the "stop" part of the process in the above scenario?

____

____

____

LOOK

What did it mean to "look" around the environment at AT&T? What did this step include?

____

____

____

____

LISTEN

Finally, how would you describe the "listen" phase and its impact?

____

____

____

____

A quick word on problem identification. Though there were plenty of problems at AT&T that needed to be solved, not all of them fell under Carly's purview and not all of them could be described as *meaningful* problems to solve.

The Experiment

Building on the idea of working to locate a *meaningful* problem to solve, consider the following problem-identification requirements:

- The problem affects me directly.
- The problem affects more people than just me.

- I have proximity to the problem.
- The problem is within my capabilities to help solve.
- I have "skin in the game" regarding this problem; for either personal or professional reasons, solving this problem is deeply important to me.

When you think of the problems that plague you today, what are a few that come to mind? (Don't overthink this; simply fire away with what comes to mind.)

1. ______________________________
2. ______________________________
3. ______________________________
4. ______________________________
5. ______________________________
6. ______________________________
7. ______________________________
8. ______________________________
9. ______________________________
10. ______________________________

From the list above, put a star next to the one problem that just won't leave you alone. It could be a financial predicament, a relational issue, an emotional struggle, a communication breakdown at work, or something else entirely. With that starred issue in mind, let's run through our five-point problem-identification grid. Check all that apply.

Does the problem you selected . . .

- affect you directly?
- affect more people than just you?
- exist in close proximity to you?
- necessitate capabilities, skills, and resources that you possess?
- stir an urgent desire in you to get it solved?

Plenty of people care deeply about the prospect of nuclear war, for example. But there are precious few people on the planet today who can enact solutions to that particular problem.

Plenty of people care deeply about seeing homelessness in our country solved. But there are only so many people who are truly close enough to the problem to resolve it once and for all.

Plenty of people care deeply about worldwide hunger, the immigration crisis, child slavery, GMOs, and a host of other issues encroaching on the health of society today, and yet most of those people are too far removed from the core of the issue to be of help.

The time may come when you find yourself in the middle of a wildly significant solution to a wildly significant problem. Indeed, there are people today who are throwing heavyweight punches at various societal scourges. But don't let *perfect* become the enemy of *good* as you set off to effect change right where you are. Yes, you need to *start.* But don't be afraid to start small. Start with the problems nearest and dearest to you, and let your impact expand from there.

Jesus didn't start out with mega-miracles, you may recall, but with life as a helpless infant. As a grown man, when he began his work, he started right where he was, focusing primarily on the relative nobodies in society—not on the powerful and prestigious of his day. With that in mind, my encouragement to you is to start with the problems nearest and dearest to you, and let your impact expand from there.

> Our tendency when we encounter problems is not exactly to rejoice. Grumble? Yes. Gripe? Of course. Gossip to anyone who will lend an ear? These are reflexive responses when troubles come our way. Running *toward* problems? Not so much. We tend to run away from them instead. Which is why, despite our griping and grumbling, our circumstances stay fixed, we remain frustrated, and not a single problem is solved.
>
> CARLY FIORINA

As we discussed, you will work through the actual solving of the problem you've chosen in later sessions. For now, consider the following upside possibilities by answering the questions below.

1. *What might the mere existence of this problem wind up teaching you about yourself?*

____

____

____

2. *What might it teach you about God?*

3. *What added capacity, insight, or skill might solving this problem produce in you?*

Albert Einstein once noted that we "cannot solve our problems with the same thinking we used when we created them." A final question, then:

4. *What stale, unhelpful thought patterns might you need to set aside in order to solve this problem?*

session 2

THE PURSUIT OF THE PATH

What Wise Leaders Know

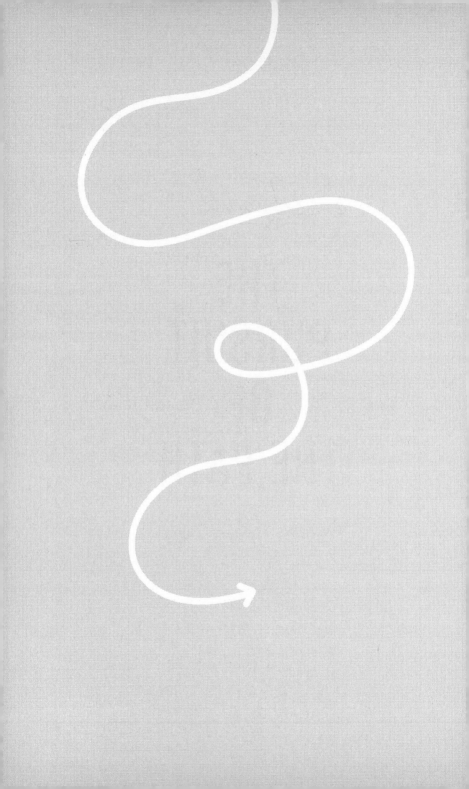

We cannot choose who we are, . . . but
we can always choose to become something more.
To stop choosing is to start dying.

Summary

While it's true that life is about solving problems that are right in front of us and around us; problems that vex us and perplex us; problems that not only drive us nuts but also challenge the sanity and stability of those in our sphere of relationships, the irony of "on-path" living is that it's not enough to spot these problems and solve them . . . there is *something more important still.*

In this session, Carly explains why the *way* we solve problems matters just as much as—if not more than—the fact that we solve them at all.

The Full Story

For more on the subjects covered in session 2, read the following chapters in *Find Your Way: Unleash Your Power and Highest Potential.*

- Chapter 4: Decisions, Decisions
- Chapter 5: What Are You Afraid Of?
- Chapter 6: Who You Are When No One's Looking
- Chapter 7: Becoming a Better *Us*
- Chapter 8: Think of the Possibilities!

First Thoughts

As you settle in, have group members answer the following question.

When you face two viable options, whether regarding which toothpaste to buy, which job to take, which relationship to pursue, or which financial plan to adopt, how do you know which one to choose?

From *Find Your Way*

To center your thoughts on this session's central topic, have a member of your group read the following excerpt aloud.

> As I dove headlong into higher education and then the workforce, I came to realize that 100 percent of leadership—both in life and in work—comes down to *choices*. Will I choose this city, or not? Take this job, or not? Befriend this person, or not? Attend this meeting, or not? Speak my mind, or not? Each decision, once made, leads to another set of choices, like branches sprawling from the trunk of a tree.
>
> The realization sobered me—so much was riding on each individual choice! But I also found it exhilarating that each crossroads mattered so much. I became a student of my own intentions, realizing that one decision, while seemingly inconsequential, could lead me either toward or away from the path I longed to be on. On this subject, author Gary Zukav has said that *intention* is the "why beneath the why." I became keenly aware of my life's sequence of whys.
>
> *Find Your Way*, PAGE 70

Video Notes

Use the space below to log notes and insights from this session's video segment.

It's all about choices

Choosing to change

What problem solving requires

Courage: "Fear not"

Courage: The fears we face

Character: The going will always get tough

Character: How you do things matters too

Character: Practice, practice, practice

Collaboration: Humility + empathy

Creatively seeing possibilities: The one leadership trait to have

Up for Discussion

Cover as many of the following discussion questions as time and group interest allow.

Power Play

1. *What concept or quote from the video segment stood out most to you, and why? Share your insights with your group.*

____

____

____

2. *The video segment mentions the importance of choices. And though there are indeed some things we cannot change—our past pain, who lives next door, our shoe size, height, and physical frame—there are plenty more things that we can change.*

Historically, which end of the spectrum below have you been on, as it relates to agency—that is, to your ability to choose? Have you been a slave to life's circumstances or someone who sees limitless options, or are you somewhere in between?

Place an X to mark your spot, and then discuss your rationale with your group.

My circumstances have always limited my options in life.	Regardless of my circumstances, I believe I can choose how things will turn out.

3. *Are you pleased with your outlook on how much choice you believe you have in life? Why or why not? What assumptions, attitudes, or firsthand experiences do you think contribute to your belief here?*

____

____

____

4. *In chapter 4 of* Find Your Way, *Carly says, "To stop choosing is to start dying." What do you think she means by this? Do you agree or disagree with her premise? Explain.*

____

____

____

> You have more power than you realize. You have probably given away that power more often than you realize.
>
> CARLY FIORINA

5. *Think of a current or recent situation where you surrendered your ability to choose, whether intentionally or unintentionally, and began to believe that you're stuck where you are, in an unfortunate set of circumstances, with no way out, with no hope and no say. What is the situation, and what about it has you feeling hamstrung?*

   Take a moment to log your thoughts, and then share your insights with the group.

____

____

____

6. *Which of the resources below do you wish you had in abundance to face down the daunting circumstances you mentioned in response to question 5?*

   - ☐ *Time*
   - ☐ *Money*
   - ☐ *Perspective*
   - ☐ *Resolve*
   - ☐ *Restraint*
   - ☐ *Control*
   - ☐ *Power*
   - ☐ *Clairvoyance*
   - ☐ *Something else:* ____________

7. *Given your situation, what do you make of the assertion that what we actually need to solve our most meaningful problems is an abundance of soul-anchored traits such as courage, collaboration, and consistency—being people who do what we say we will do?*

____

____

____

> It isn't enough to merely *see* the problem. And it isn't even enough to *solve* the problem. To reach your fullest potential, you must also understand that *how* you solve the problem is just as important as solving it.
>
> CARLY FIORINA

Not Just the What, but the How

1. *Describe a time when you could relate to the "if only" scenarios mentioned in the video, the extrinsic dilemmas that seem to hold the key to our feeling at peace. The original list from* Find Your Way *appears below. Select one of those five options, or come up with one of your own.*

    - *"If only people would stop saying those things about me . . ."*
    - *"If only my boss could see the value I add . . ."*
    - *"If only I could afford that resource . . ."*
    - *"If only I'd had those opportunities . . ."*
    - *"If only I'd had that kind of time . . ."*
    - *"If only ______________________________."*

2. *How might developing inner-world traits such as courage and character give you back some of the power you feel your circumstances have taken from you?*

____

____

____

3. *Do you agree or disagree with the assertion that developing the following four character traits is 100 percent within our control? Why?*

- Courage: *the ability to rightly put fear in its place.*
- Character: *the manifestation of integrity—integrated living—over time.*
- Collaboration: *effectively coming together with others who care about solving the same problem as you.*
- Creatively seeing possibilities: *the ability to look beyond our circumstances, no matter how harrowing.*

> We can get better at getting better, refusing to settle for who we are today, but always pressing on to who we can become.
>
> CARLY FIORINA

To glean lessons regarding each of the character traits explored in this session, we'll look at a biblical parable from Jesus' teachings, an anecdote from Carly's leadership experience, and an example from your own life as a leader. For each category, have different group members read the excerpts. Then answer the questions that follow.

A Word on Courage

THE PARABLE: THE WISE AND FOOLISH BUILDERS

Near the end of his Sermon on the Mount, Jesus instructs his disciples to be careful to build their lives on a solid foundation:

> "Anyone who listens to my teaching and follows it is wise, like a person who builds a house on solid rock. Though the rain comes in torrents and the floodwaters rise and the winds beat against that house, it won't collapse because it is built on bedrock. But anyone who hears my teaching and doesn't obey it is foolish, like a person who builds a house on sand. When the rains and floods come and the winds beat against that house, it will collapse with a mighty crash."
>
> When Jesus had finished saying these things, the crowds were amazed at his teaching, for he taught with real authority—quite unlike their teachers of religious law.
>
> MATTHEW 7:24-29

THE ANECDOTE: GLEN THE LAWYER

In chapter 5 of *Find Your Way*, Carly writes about an occasion early in her career when she desperately needed courage. She was overseeing a team of engineers who were asked to provide detailed information about an internal legal dispute to one of the company's attorneys on a weekly basis.

> Whenever Glen the Lawyer called someone on my staff to make a request, instead of handling the exchange like a normal, civilized human being, he would yell and scream and often hang up on my team member. He was incredibly abusive, and I got quite an earful from my colleagues every time they received a call from Glen. One day, I'd finally had enough.

I picked up the phone, dialed Glen's number, and told him, "You may not treat my team this way."

"Respect for the individual" was one of our core values at AT&T, and the members of my team were not being respected.

"Glen," I continued, "you need to be respectful of these people. They are working hard for you. They're jumping through all your hoops, in addition to doing their normal jobs. They deserve better than how you're treating them."

Glen the Lawyer was much higher in the organization than I was, which is perhaps why he wasn't too pleased with my telling him what he needed to do. I knew he wasn't happy because he expressed his displeasure right then and there, over the phone. In mostly four-letter words. He ended his verbal rampage with a question: "What are you going to do about it?"

It seemed I had stumbled upon a crossroads, and I knew I had a decision to make. *I can either lend power to courage*, I thought, *or else give power to my fear*.

"Glen," I said, "unless and until you apologize and behave differently, we will no longer do work for you."

With that, I hung up the phone. And then I burst into tears. I may have lent power to courage on the outside, but inside I was a bundle of fear. After several moments of wondering what on earth I'd just done, I composed myself, walked out to where my team sat, and told them what I'd said to Glen. I instructed them not to do an ounce of work for him until further notice.

"I may have just gotten myself fired," I told them, "but I stand by what I've done. If you catch any heat from this, you make me the bad guy. Understood?"

Heads nodded and lips drew up into subtle grins. Nobody likes to be bullied. Nobody likes to be treated like scum. Glen the Lawyer had been put in his place, and even though my knees were knocking, I knew I had done the right thing.

It took Glen another two days before he fully got the message and called to apologize. But to his credit, he apologized to my team, and he apologized to me. Best of all, he made all future requests for information graciously, and my team was happy to comply.

Find Your Way, PAGES 83–84

YOUR OWN STORY

Now it's your turn. Describe a recent occasion when you demonstrated courage in a work-related dealing. What was the situation, and why was courage required? How did things pan out for you in the end? Capture your thoughts on the lines below before moving on to the questions.

1. *Thinking back on the biblical parable about the wise and foolish builders, and on Carly's example of demonstrating courage with Glen the Lawyer, what are the parallels you see between the two stories?*

____

____

____

2. *When do you feel most challenged to exhibit courage? What situations tend to stir up feelings of fear?*

____

____

____

3. *Adding your own story into the mix, what benefit(s) accrued—in Jesus' parable, in Carly's example, in your own life—because someone manifested courage?*

____

____

____

Character Matters

THE PARABLE: THE THREE SERVANTS

Just after telling his disciples about what future days held for believers in him, Jesus offered up a pair of parables, one about preparedness and this one, about responsibility:

> The Kingdom of Heaven can be illustrated by the story of a man going on a long trip. He called

together his servants and entrusted his money to them while he was gone. He gave five bags of silver to one, two bags of silver to another, and one bag of silver to the last—dividing it in proportion to their abilities. He then left on his trip.

The servant who received the five bags of silver began to invest the money and earned five more. The servant with two bags of silver also went to work and earned two more. But the servant who received the one bag of silver dug a hole in the ground and hid the master's money.

After a long time their master returned from his trip and called them to give an account of how they had used his money. The servant to whom he had entrusted the five bags of silver came forward with five more and said, "Master, you gave me five bags of silver to invest, and I have earned five more."

The master was full of praise. "Well done, my good and faithful servant. You have been faithful in handling this small amount, so now I will give you many more responsibilities. Let's celebrate together!"

The servant who had received the two bags of silver came forward and said, "Master, you gave me two bags of silver to invest, and I have earned two more."

The master said, "Well done, my good and faithful servant. You have been faithful in handling this small amount, so now I will give you many more responsibilities. Let's celebrate together!"

Then the servant with the one bag of silver came

and said, "Master, I knew you were a harsh man, harvesting crops you didn't plant and gathering crops you didn't cultivate. I was afraid I would lose your money, so I hid it in the earth. Look, here is your money back."

But the master replied, "You wicked and lazy servant! If you knew I harvested crops I didn't plant and gathered crops I didn't cultivate, why didn't you deposit my money in the bank? At least I could have gotten some interest on it."

Then he ordered, "Take the money from this servant, and give it to the one with the ten bags of silver. To those who use well what they are given, even more will be given, and they will have an abundance. But from those who do nothing, even what little they have will be taken away. Now throw this useless servant into outer darkness, where there will be weeping and gnashing of teeth."

MATTHEW 25:14-30

THE ANECDOTE: CANCER SUFFERERS

I spent the majority of 2009 battling breast cancer, and I met plenty of people involved in that same fight who displayed great strength of character. Despite the pain, uncertainty, and disillusionment that accompany that disease, these people did not give in to despair. They showed up, with hope alive in their hearts and words of encouragement on their lips, determined to finish strong, regardless of the outcome. Their strength of character—their

determination to keep moving forward—had a profound effect on me. It made it easier for me to be hopeful, encouraging, and determined.
Find Your Way, PAGE 110

YOUR OWN STORY

Before you address the following questions, think about a time—a recent one, if possible—when you reaped the benefits of having displayed *character*—that is, "Real integrity. Proven over time." Jot down your thoughts on the lines below.

THE APPLICATION

1. *What role does the concept of time play, both in the parable of the three servants and in Carly's story of fellow cancer sufferers? Why is time a necessary component when evaluating someone's character—including your own?*

2. *The video segment acknowledges the difficulty in defining character. For her father, character meant things such as candor, integrity, and standing up for what you believe. How do you put words to what the concept of character means?*

____

____

____

____

3. *On the grid below, note times when you've seen the various truths about character play out in your own experience.*

FOUR TRUTHS ABOUT CHARACTER

CHARACTER TRUTH	HOW YOU'VE SEEN THIS TRUTH PLAY OUT
☐ **No. 1:** Character is critical when the going gets tough. (And the going always gets tough.)	
☐ **No. 2:** Contrary to popular opinion, the ends never justify the means.	
☐ **No. 3:** Character demands reflection, and reflection can't be rushed.	
☐ **No. 4:** The more we manifest strength of character, the stronger our character becomes.	

4. *What other truths about character have you learned along the way? Did the lesson(s) come easily to you, or did you learn the hard way?*

____

____

____

> Once we dive into the task of solving meaningful problems, we realize that things will never be as smooth or straightforward as we imagined them to be—despite even the most careful planning. It won't be as fun. It won't be as exciting. It won't be as victorious as we dreamed. Which is why long-term courage is required. It's not just that we're getting the ball rolling; most times, it's that we're rolling the ball *uphill*.
>
> CARLY FIORINA

People Who Need People

THE PARABLE: THE PRODIGAL SON

Hitting his disciples with multiple lessons at once, Jesus delivers three parables in a row in Luke 15, all of them dealing with things that were once lost but now are found. First, a sheep; next, a precious coin; and finally, a beloved son . . . what parent wouldn't grieve that?

> To illustrate the point further, Jesus told them [his disciples] this story: "A man had two sons. The younger son told his father, 'I want my share of your

estate now before you die.' So his father agreed to divide his wealth between his sons.

"A few days later this younger son packed all his belongings and moved to a distant land, and there he wasted all his money in wild living. About the time his money ran out, a great famine swept over the land, and he began to starve. He persuaded a local farmer to hire him, and the man sent him into his fields to feed the pigs. The young man became so hungry that even the pods he was feeding the pigs looked good to him. But no one gave him anything.

"When he finally came to his senses, he said to himself, 'At home even the hired servants have food enough to spare, and here I am dying of hunger! I will go home to my father and say, "Father, I have sinned against both heaven and you, and I am no longer worthy of being called your son. Please take me on as a hired servant."'

"So he returned home to his father. And while he was still a long way off, his father saw him coming. Filled with love and compassion, he ran to his son, embraced him, and kissed him. His son said to him, 'Father, I have sinned against both heaven and you, and I am no longer worthy of being called your son.'

"But his father said to the servants, 'Quick! Bring the finest robe in the house and put it on him. Get a ring for his finger and sandals for his feet. And kill the calf we have been fattening. We must celebrate with a feast, for this son of mine was dead and has now returned to life. He was lost, but now he is found.' So the party began.

"Meanwhile, the older son was in the fields working. When he returned home, he heard music and dancing in the house, and he asked one of the servants what was going on. 'Your brother is back,' he was told, 'and your father has killed the fattened calf. We are celebrating because of his safe return.'

"The older brother was angry and wouldn't go in. His father came out and begged him, but he replied, 'All these years I've slaved for you and never once refused to do a single thing you told me to. And in all that time you never gave me even one young goat for a feast with my friends. Yet when this son of yours comes back after squandering your money on prostitutes, you celebrate by killing the fattened calf!'

"His father said to him, 'Look, dear son, you have always stayed by me, and everything I have is yours. We had to celebrate this happy day. For your brother was dead and has come back to life! He was lost, but now he is found!'"

LUKE 15:11-9, 22-32

THE ANECDOTE: A SURPRISING RESOLUTION TO THE STRIP CLUB STORY

You remember the story of my first client meeting, at the strip club in Washington, DC—the fear I had to overcome; the embarrassment I faced upon entering the club; my horror at watching my colleague, Carl, call women over to do table dances for our client; my utter relief when those women demurred. Well, hours after I returned to the office that day, Carl came sauntering in. No doubt emboldened by the drinks he'd enjoyed over lunch, he walked by my desk, slipped a black garter he'd obtained from one of the dancers onto my coffee mug, and walked on without saying a word.

Once Carl was out of earshot, the man who shared office space with me looked up from his work and said, "That guy's got no class."

I met my colleague's eyes but said nothing. Carl's gesture had said it all. But I did take note of the fact that Carl wasn't as bulletproof as I'd believed. Here was one of his peers subtly distancing himself from Carl; did others in the office feel the same way?

Carl never once brought up the strip-club lunch, but as I mentioned, he started treating me with respect. I suppose that in the same way a fraternity pledge must survive hazing to get into the frat's good graces, I had to live through The Board Room for Carl to know I was there to stay.

About nine months into my tenure in that role at AT&T, Carl approached me and said, "You know, Carly, this isn't such a bad arrangement we've got going here . . ."

The "arrangement" he was referring to was the pattern he and I had established for working clients together. Carl would reel in the new business, and I made sure their telecom needs were fulfilled. Carl's sweet spot was relationships. He had all the right connections and was really good at schmoozing decision makers. Where he lacked expertise was in following through on the clients' actual needs. They had real problems needing to be solved, problems that couldn't be addressed by good ol' boy drinking sprees and table dances—problems that I became equipped and eager to help solve. . . .

Young women ask me all the time for the "one piece of advice" I'd give them as they enter the workforce. Without exception, I say, "Never hide your light under a bushel basket, and never get a chip on your shoulder." In our context here, we might say it like this: Be proud of the power you wield in this world, and watch for ways to share it with others for the greater good—in your own time, in your own way, and on your own terms.

Find Your Way, PAGES 159–161

YOUR OWN STORY

When have you bumped into a situation that demanded collaboration from you? What did you decide to do, and how did your decision serve you—or not—in the end? Capture the thoughts that come to mind here before moving on.

THE APPLICATION

1. *Do you agree or disagree with Carly's decision to work with Carl instead of against him in the end? Would you have made the same decision, or a different one? Why?*

> As we seek to stay the course toward our fullest potential, while keeping our feet firmly planted on the path, it's one thing to master our inner world—overcoming fear, manifesting courage, carving out time for earnest reflection, sticking to our values when the going gets tough—but it's another thing entirely to master these skills in our outward relationships.
>
> CARLY FIORINA

2. *What has collaboration cost you along the way? On the flip side, what have you gained?*

3. *What do you make of the assertion from this session's video segment that "nothing of lasting value happens with an individual person acting alone"? Explain your thoughts to the group.*

Realism + Optimism = Useful Creativity

THE PARABLE: THE PERSISTENT WIDOW

One day, Jesus told his disciples about the value of seeing possibilities, of never giving up, of fighting for a better tomorrow than what reality is like today.

> "There was a judge in a certain city," [Jesus] said, "who neither feared God nor cared about people. A widow of that city came to him repeatedly, saying, 'Give me justice in this dispute with my enemy.' The judge ignored her for a while, but finally he said to himself, 'I don't fear God or care about people, but this woman is driving me crazy. I'm going to see that she gets justice, because she is wearing me out with her constant requests!'"
>
> Then the Lord said, "Learn a lesson from this unjust judge. Even he rendered a just decision in the end. So don't you think God will surely give justice to his chosen people who cry out to him day and night? Will he keep putting them off? I tell you, he will grant justice to them quickly! But when the Son

of Man returns, how many will he find on the earth who have faith?"

LUKE 18:2-8

THE ANECDOTE: JEFFREY AND GREG

Recently, another of my colleagues, Jeffrey, faced a dilemma. . . . Jeffrey is a deep thinker with a quick wit, an expansive heart, and a hearty laugh. He's delightful to be around. As our director of coaching, Jeffrey is well-versed in all our problem-solving tools. This came in handy when a young man he knows (I'll call him Greg) encountered some problems. Jeffrey knew right where to start.

Greg had long dreamed of going to culinary school, so it was a big deal when, upon graduation from high school, he was accepted to ICC, the International Culinary Center in New York City. His parents coughed up tens of thousands of dollars for the young man to turn his dream into reality; but as we've seen, such destination-minded thinking often leaves us longing for more.

Greg arrived in New York and registered for classes, but he soon realized he had made a mistake. He missed the opportunity to take one class altogether and had to drop a second class because he hadn't taken the prerequisite yet. When his first-year schedule was found lacking by the school's administrators, they issued him his first "ding."

Soon thereafter, he was caught drinking in the dorm—his second ding.

What he didn't know but was about to find out the hard way was that at a highly selective school like ICC, it's two dings and you're out. Greg was expelled from the program of his dreams, and the fees he had paid were not refundable. He was furious. His parents were furious. Now what was he supposed to do?

Grudgingly, he packed up his dorm room, headed back to his parents' house, and got a job waiting tables. If he couldn't attend culinary school, at least he could do something in the food-service industry. Before long, however, living at home became too much to bear, and he decided to move out of his parents' house. He had recently started dating a young woman, and she agreed to let him move in with her.

Jeffrey said that this is where things really began to careen downhill.

"Greg quit his job at the restaurant because he didn't think he was making enough money. But at least it was a job. At least it was a paycheck. He had nowhere else to go!"

He had been paying rent to his girlfriend, so when the paychecks stopped coming in, she kicked him out.

"Eventually, I had trouble reaching him," Jeffrey said, "and then I found out why. His girlfriend had bought his phone for him—and she kept it for herself when they broke up."

So now Greg had no culinary-school degree, no job, no place to live, and no phone. Things were not looking good.

It would have been easy for Jeffrey to leave this

kid to find his own way; but knowing that so much of unlocking our own potential involves helping others unlock theirs . . . , Jeffrey ran toward Greg instead of running away.

"His current state was obvious to both of us," Jeffrey said. "He was hanging out with the wrong crowd, blowing his time and money on stuff that could wreck his life, and believing things about himself that were complete and utter lies. We both agreed on the current state.

"The future state? That was tougher to pin down. I could see a future for this kid that he couldn't yet see for himself. All he saw was further struggle, further disappointment, further hopelessness, further pain. But I knew he was talented. I knew he had gifts. I knew he could build a valuable life for himself. I knew he could win. As far as I was concerned, my role was to bring into view the future state that I knew for sure could be his."

Jeffrey began having weekly conversations with Greg (who, fortunately, had bought a new phone), during which he prompted the young man to articulate his desired future state.

"I simply kept asking questions," Jeffrey said, which by now you know I think is a pretty fantastic place to start.

Jeffrey would ask him, "The dynamics you're facing—are they what you hoped would be true of you at this stage in your life?"

Greg would moan and say, "No."

"What dynamics would you like to be true for you, then?"

Greg didn't have an immediate answer for that.

When new drama entered the equation, Jeffrey asked Greg, "How's that working for you?"

When Greg's friends would drag him away from becoming the man he said he wanted to be, Jeffrey would ask, "What types of friends do you want to attract, and what are the implications of that for the person you want to become?"

It took a long time, but eventually Greg went from borrowing Jeffrey's beliefs about his future to buying into those beliefs himself.

"We're still hard at work," Jeffrey recently told me. "And we will be for quite some time. But I'm convinced that as Greg and I keep speaking aloud his desired future state and he assumes the task of becoming the kind of person for whom that future state is a reality, he'll get there."

I believe Jeffrey is right. Regardless of what a person—any person—has or hasn't done, simply planting his or her feet on the path begins to unlock potential.

Find Your Way, PAGES 173–176

YOUR OWN STORY

When have you felt compelled to go all out toward a vision of the future that nobody else seemed to see? Why was the urging so strong? What became of the situation? What became of you? Note your thoughts on the lines below before moving ahead.

THE APPLICATION

1. *If you were to compare Carly's anecdote to the parable of the persistent widow, who do you think is the judge, and who do you think is the widow? What similarities do you see?*

2. *In any of the above three stories—the biblical parable, Carly's anecdote, or your firsthand account—what role did persistence play? How persistent a person are you when it comes to balancing the very real nature of your present life circumstances with what's possible?*

3. *You'll have an opportunity to work through this material on a more personal level in the between-sessions work, but for now, think of the one trait mentioned in this session that you'd like to improve. Is it courage? Character? Collaboration? The ability to see creative possibilities?*

____

____

____

Consider your answer to that question. Then, respond to the invitation below.

Now Go (and Grow)

Before dismissing your gathering, ask each member of the group how he or she plans to implement the following action steps.

1. *Solicit input. Confirm your hunches regarding how effectively and consistently you manifest the traits discussed in this session by asking a trusted friend for help. Ask:*
   - *How fearful or courageous do you find me to be? Do I tend to fret over things that are outside of my control, or do you observe me turning and facing challenging situations head-on?*
   - *Do you believe that I'm a person of strong character? What conversations or shared experiences inform your perceptions here?*
   - *How collaborative would you say I am? Do you suspect that I'd rather fly solo than work in the context of a team? Or do you find that I'm forever including other people, checking my assumptions with colleagues, and refusing to go it alone?*

- *Do you think I cling to negative circumstances too tightly, forgetting that I can make choices that will bring about helpful change? Or do you think I neglect to adequately weigh "the way things are" and instead have my head perpetually in the clouds? Do you think I balance the two?*

2. *Submit yourself to growth. Once you have a bit of feedback in hand, consider how you might practice the one trait you are trying to improve. Often, simply putting a desire in mind, such as "I'd like to practice mustering courage this week," can reorient your entire world, such that you're more likely to see positive results.*

> No matter how rough the streets, no matter how loud the cries, no matter how deep the pain, no matter how dark the night, the power that resides inside you is greater than the power of the circumstances that threaten your joy.
>
> CARLY FIORINA

Looking for More?

To dive deeper into the concepts presented in session 2, complete the following section on your own, before your next group meeting.

In this "Looking for More?" section, you will dig deeper on an extended excerpt from the book *Find Your Way*, engage with a few evaluative and introspective exercises, and experiment with applying the core concepts to your life.

The Excerpt

In chapter 6 of *Find Your Way*, Carly elaborates on a practice that helps us strengthen not only our character, but also any other inner-world trait. The practice is *reflection*—self-assessment that is earnest, thorough, and paced.

> To reach our potential in developing our character, we must carve out time for reflection, for review, for insight. We must ask ourselves the questions no one else will ask us: How well did we live up to our values today? How did we spend our time when we were alone? How did we add value to those we encountered? Are we pleased by the actions we took? . . .
>
> For many years now, my practice has included waking in the early-morning hours—to sit, to pray, to think. I've found that if it doesn't happen then, it doesn't happen at all. Once I'm engaged in the day's work, I tend not to slow down as the day wears on. . . .

I'm not handing you an expectation as much as an *invitation*: Pull back from your usual obligations—for an hour, ten minutes, three breaths. Reflect on the day you've just finished or the one you're about to begin; think about the conversations you've had, the flashes of insight that rushed through your mind. Sit with those thoughts and explore what they mean. Turn them over in your mind like gems. Invest a commute, or a walk, or a bath as a time for simple reflection. Take up journaling. Practice prayer. After you've tried this a few times, see if you don't feel more centered, more gracious, more aligned with your desired self. See if you're beginning to approach interactions with others differently, as one who is more patient, more open, more at ease. See if you don't make key decisions differently, now that you've added a boost of thoughtfulness to your world.

Find Your Way, PAGES 121–123

The Evaluation

1. *What doubts or fears surface in your mind as you consider Carly's words?*

___

___

___

2. *Which aspects of Carly's exhortation seem at least somewhat doable to you, and why? In other words, if you were to name*

a starting point for this practice of self-reflection, what might that initial step include?

3. *What do you suspect you would gain from instituting a practice of self-reflection? How might such a practice help in your problem-solving endeavors?*

The Experiment

Give self-reflection a try. Sometime during your day, carve out twenty minutes—or an hour, if you're able—and complete the prompts that begin on page 70. Then read the questions that follow, noting your answers here in this guide or simply carrying the questions with you as you come to the end of your day.

> Keep your wits about you. Stay true to your values. Stand down in the face of impulsivity. Refuse the temptation to do, do, do, respond, respond, respond. You will not regret this measured approach, I promise you. You're bringing sanity back to your life.
>
> CARLY FIORINA

Today, I upheld *these* values that I say matter to me:

____

____

Today, I *neglected to uphold* these values that I say matter to me:

____

____

What my attitude today says about me:

____

____

What my actions today say about me:

____

____

I demonstrated *humility* today when . . .

____

____

I demonstrated *empathy* today when . . .

____

____

I demonstrated *courage* today when . . .

____

____

I demonstrated *a collaborative spirit* today when . . .

____

____

Today I chose to see *creative possibilities* instead of possible setbacks when . . .

____

____

Here is an ongoing problem that I need help solving:

____

____

The aspect of life requiring the most courage from me right now is . . .

____

____

In *Find Your Way*, Carly suggests that the right decisions for us are ones that serve our highest purposes—not just today, but long into the future. With that idea in mind, reflect on the following three questions before moving on. If you'd like, journal your thoughts in the space provided below.

1. How do I feel about who I am in this era of my life?
2. How do I feel about who I am becoming in this era of my life?
3. Ten years from now, what do I hope to see as I look back on this present era?

session 3

THE PROMISE OF THE PATH

Problem Solvers, Unite!

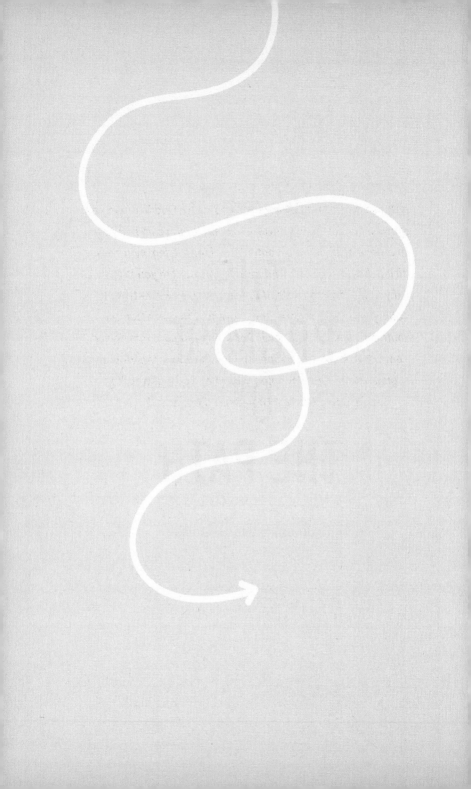

In the same way that I will never know anything but being a woman, I believe I will never know anything besides trying to always operate at full potential—ideas flying, cylinders firing, heart engaged. And my commitment to you is this: If you will devote yourself to the practices we've talked about—the perspective, the courage, the character, the whole bit—you too will never know anything but maximized potential. If you will choose to live this way, I can all but guarantee that a day will come when you will wonder,

When's the last time I wasn't content?

Summary

Your purpose on this earth is to solve problems. In fact, when you encounter the problems that *you* were made to solve, it confirms you're on the right path. So problem solving is key. But as we discovered in the previous session, *how* you go about solving those problems is every bit as important as the much-needed solutions you bring. Now, bring on the problems, right?

Far too often, even once we're on board with a problem-solving way of life, when it comes to executing against this deeply held desire, our eyes glaze over as ideas run dry. How does one *actually* solve a problem? What steps must a person take?

In this third and final session, Carly explains the four aspects of her signature Leadership Framework, an approach that has helped hundreds of leaders in all sectors of society solve the problems they were meant to solve.

The Full Story

For more on the subjects covered in session 3, read the following chapters in *Find Your Way: Unleash Your Power and Highest Potential.*

- Chapter 9: No Gimmes Here: Promise No. 1: Problems Will Get Solved
- Chapter 10: To-the-Brim Living: Promise No. 2: Potential Will Be Unleashed

First Thoughts

As you settle in, have group members answer the following questions.

- If you could wave a magic wand and solve one problem in your world today, what problem would you solve?

- Why is this problem so frustrating to you? How has it affected you along the way?

From *Find Your Way*

To center your thoughts on this session's central topic, have a member of your group read the following excerpt aloud.

> This idea that problems are the pavement under our feet, the very thing that tells us we're on the right path, is not just lip service for me. It's how I live my life. Solving problems is what we were made for, remember?
>
> We see beauty and are moved to capture it.
> We see need and are moved to meet it.
> We see suffering and are moved to eradicate it.
> We see hope and are moved to multiply it.
> We see love and are moved to return it.
> We see joy and are moved to relish it.
> We see pain and are moved to alleviate it.
> We see peril and are moved to avoid it.
> We see grace and are moved to reflect it.
>
> Yes, we get tired and frustrated. Yes, we can be harsh with our words. Yes, distractions still tempt us. Yes, we think our way is best. But at the core of who we are, we're focused on making things better. We're determined to learn, to change, to grow. That's

why certain problems make your heart beat faster, make you long to jump into the fray. You were made for solving those problems. You have the needed resources to solve those problems. You owe it to yourself and others to play through.

Find Your Way, PAGES 214–215

Video Notes

Use the space below to log notes and insights from this session's video segment.

The group for whom this approach will not work

What change requires

Slacktivism as substitute

Defining the goal

Step by step . . .

What gets measured gets done

What's the culture like around here?

The dreaded querencia

"That look is fuel."

On playing through

Up for Discussion

Cover as many of the following discussion questions as time and group interest allow.

The Opposite of a Problem Solver

1. *What concepts stood out to you in this session's video segment, and why?*

2. *Early in the video segment, Frank and Carly allude to a group for whom the problem-solving tools—choosing path over plan; choosing courage, character, and collaboration; looking for creative possibilities—rarely work. When have you encountered someone who seemingly didn't want to see problems get solved? What was it like to relate with this person? What do you suppose motivated his or her inactive stance?*

3. *When have you felt a little more passion for griping about a problem than jumping in to help solve it? What motivated your own inactive stance?*

Not Quite Problem Solving, but Still . . .

1. *What do you make of the pervasive societal trend toward slacktivism? What noble intent might be behind these efforts? On the flip side, what harm might slacktivism cause?*

> I am not saying that nothing good comes from raising awareness by hopping on the bandwagon, hashtagging our support for causes, and pumping our fists and shouting, "Things must change!" I'm simply suggesting that if we want to see meaningful change, if we want to create substantive and lasting solutions to the very real problems we face, . . . we must *see*, *listen*, *learn*, and *work*.
>
> CARLY FIORINA

2. *On your life's journey thus far, how activistic have you been along the way? What causes have stirred you to action, and what outcomes resulted from your work? Take a few minutes to log your thoughts on the lines below before sharing your insights with the group.*

3. *What would it look like to go beyond fist-pumping activism to "see, listen, learn, and work"?*

____

____

____

____

____

4. *According to the following Scripture passages, what resources are Christ-followers promised in life? Which do you think are necessary for problem solving?*

James 1:5 _______________

____

Psalm 119:105 _______________

____

Proverbs 3:5-6 _______________

____

Philippians 4:13 _______________

____

Ephesians 4:23 _______________

____

1 John 4:19 _______________

____

5. *It doesn't take a rocket scientist to understand the Leadership Framework, yet too often people fail to think through these basic problem-solving categories. Can you relate? Give an example of a time when you launched into problem-solving mode before mapping out a thoughtful plan. What was the problem? What did your efforts involve? What happened in the end?*

As you plot your own supporting steps, keep in mind that you may not be able to name all of them right away. Even so, I'll bet you can identify one or two to get you started. Between you and your problem-solving compatriots, my guess is you'll know more than you think you do. Here's a simple prompt: What do we not have today that we'll need—to either innovate, build, or acquire? Let your answer to that question drive your steps.

CARLY FIORINA

The Foundation of Every Worthwhile Solution

1. *What do you make of the theory that "when trying to solve problems in an organization or group, we can become so overwhelmed by the complexity of what we're trying to do that we begin to shortchange or neglect certain things, or we focus only on the aspects of problem solving that we truly enjoy"?*

2. *For the sake of confirming what at some level you already know, which aspect of the following problem-solving process are you most likely to gravitate toward, and which are you likely to avoid? Place X's on the aspects you tend to disregard and check marks on the aspects you most enjoy.*

   - ☐ *Spotting the problem.*
   - ☐ *Announcing that "we have a problem."*
   - ☐ *Defining the problem.*
   - ☐ *Delineating the steps necessary to solve the problem.*
   - ☐ *Recruiting others to the problem-solving effort.*
   - ☐ *Establishing and maintaining a positive problem-solving culture.*
   - ☐ *Measuring progress along the way.*
   - ☐ *Solving the problem.*

3. *Of the common reasons cited in the video segment for skimming over certain aspects of problem solving, which do you most relate to, and why? Select one from the list below and share your insights with the group.*

   - *Fear of change: "Change requires an investment—of attention, of time, of energy, of strength. For some people, the investment seems way too big."*
   - *Lack of motivation: "Another reason that problem perceivers refuse to become problem solvers is that the pain simply isn't that bad."*
   - *The allure of slacktivism: "People pretend to be engaged in something important, something that looks like problem solving, even as they do nothing of substance or permanence to support the cause."*
   - *Lack of know-how: "Sometimes we just don't know where to start . . . [and] the natural first response is to feel completely overwhelmed."*

4. *Whenever Carly is faced with a problem, she uses a tool she created called the Leadership Framework. It begins with four broad categories that simply must be addressed if we're going to solve our problem, and if that solution is truly going to stick. Based on the prompts below, jot down your understanding from the video segment of each of the four parts of the Leadership Framework. In other words, what must be accomplished in each of the following four phases?*

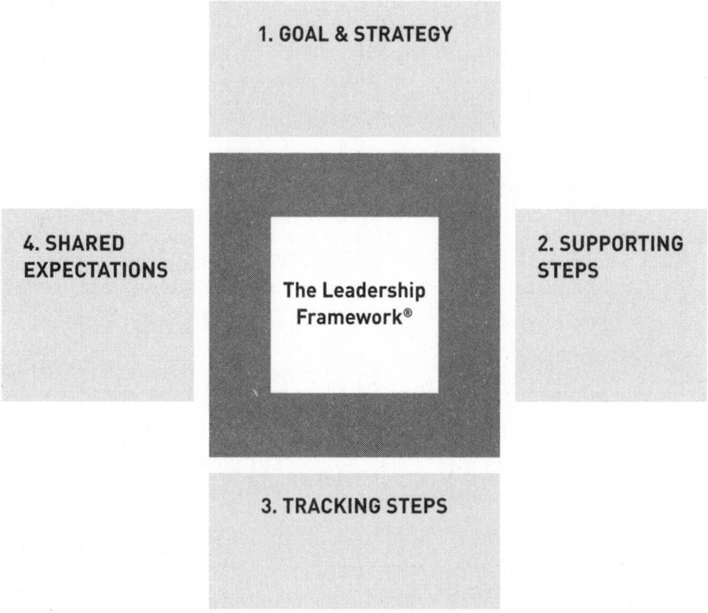

5. *Just over two thousand years ago, Jesus launched what is perhaps the greatest, most significant problem-solving effort the world will ever know, in the establishment and commissioning of the local church. Review the "project summary" below and answer the questions that follow.*

The Launch of the Local Church

Then the eleven disciples left for Galilee, going to the mountain where Jesus had told them to go. When they saw him, they worshiped him—but some of them doubted!

Jesus came and told his disciples, "I have been given all authority in heaven and on earth. Therefore, go and make disciples of all the nations, baptizing them in the name of the Father and the Son and the Holy Spirit. Teach these new disciples to obey all the commands I have given you. And be sure of this: I am with you always, even to the end of the age."

MATTHEW 28:16-20

In my first book I told you, Theophilus, about everything Jesus began to do and teach until the day he was taken up to heaven after giving his chosen apostles further instructions through the Holy Spirit. During the forty days after he suffered and died, he appeared to the apostles from time to time, and he proved to them in many ways that he was actually alive. And he talked to them about the Kingdom of God.

Once when he was eating with them, he commanded them, "Do not leave Jerusalem until the

Father sends you the gift he promised, as I told you before. John baptized with water, but in just a few days you will be baptized with the Holy Spirit."

So when the apostles were with Jesus, they kept asking him, "Lord, has the time come for you to free Israel and restore our kingdom?"

He replied, "The Father alone has the authority to set those dates and times, and they are not for you to know. But you will receive power when the Holy Spirit comes upon you. And you will be my witnesses, telling people about me everywhere—in Jerusalem, throughout Judea, in Samaria, and to the ends of the earth." . . .

On the day of Pentecost all the believers were meeting together in one place. Suddenly, there was a sound from heaven like the roaring of a mighty windstorm, and it filled the house where they were sitting. Then, what looked like flames or tongues of fire appeared and settled on each of them. And everyone present was filled with the Holy Spirit and began speaking in other languages, as the Holy Spirit gave them this ability.

At that time there were devout Jews from every nation living in Jerusalem. When they heard the loud noise, everyone came running, and they were bewildered to hear their own languages being spoken by the believers.

They were completely amazed. "How can this be?" they exclaimed. "These people are all from Galilee, and yet we hear them speaking in our own native languages! Here we are—Parthians, Medes, Elamites, people from Mesopotamia, Judea, Cappadocia, Pontus, the province of Asia, Phrygia, Pamphylia, Egypt, and the areas of Libya around Cyrene, visitors from Rome (both Jews and converts to Judaism), Cretans, and Arabs. And we all hear these people speaking in our own languages about the wonderful things God has done!" They stood there amazed and perplexed. "What can this mean?" they asked each other.

But others in the crowd ridiculed them, saying, "They're just drunk, that's all!"

Then Peter stepped forward with the eleven other apostles and shouted to the crowd, "Listen carefully, all of you, fellow Jews and residents of Jerusalem! Make no mistake about this. These people are not drunk, as some of you are assuming. Nine o'clock in the morning is much too early for that. No, what you see was predicted long ago by the prophet Joel:

'In the last days,' God says,
  'I will pour out my Spirit upon all people.
Your sons and daughters will prophesy.
  Your young men will see visions,
  and your old men will dream dreams.
In those days I will pour out my Spirit
  even on my servants—men and women alike—
  and they will prophesy.
And I will cause wonders in the heavens above

and signs on the earth below—
blood and fire and clouds of smoke.
The sun will become dark,
and the moon will turn blood red
before that great and glorious day of the LORD
arrives.
But everyone who calls on the name of the LORD
will be saved.'" . . .

Peter's words pierced their hearts, and they said to him and to the other apostles, "Brothers, what should we do?"

Peter replied, "Each of you must repent of your sins and turn to God, and be baptized in the name of Jesus Christ for the forgiveness of your sins. Then you will receive the gift of the Holy Spirit. This promise is to you, to your children, and to those far away—all who have been called by the Lord our God." Then Peter continued preaching for a long time, strongly urging all his listeners, "Save yourselves from this crooked generation!"

Those who believed what Peter said were baptized and added to the church that day—about 3,000 in all.

All the believers devoted themselves to the apostles' teaching, and to fellowship, and to sharing in meals (including the Lord's Supper), and to prayer.

A deep sense of awe came over them all, and

the apostles performed many miraculous signs and wonders. And all the believers met together in one place and shared everything they had. They sold their property and possessions and shared the money with those in need. They worshiped together at the Temple each day, met in homes for the Lord's Supper, and shared their meals with great joy and generosity—all the while praising God and enjoying the goodwill of all the people. And each day the Lord added to their fellowship those who were being saved.

ACTS 1:1-8; 2:1-21, 37-47

1. *How would you encapsulate the goal and strategy behind this local-church initiative?*

___

___

___

2. *In terms of how this goal would be accomplished, what do you see as the project's supporting steps?*

a. ___

b. ___

c. ___

d. ___

e. ___

f. ___

3. *What tracking steps were attached to this project of winning the whole world for Jesus?*

4. *How would you characterize the shared expectations Jesus intended here?*

5. *How would you describe the project's success, in light of two-thousand-plus years of development and action?*

6. *In session 2, we looked at the story of Jeffrey and his young friend Greg, who needed help putting his life back together after getting kicked out of culinary school. After rereading the account below, from* Find Your Way, *see if you can spot the four key categories from the Leadership Framework.*

The Story of Jeffrey and Greg

Recently, another of my colleagues, Jeffrey, faced a dilemma. . . . Jeffrey is a deep thinker, with a quick wit, an expansive heart, and a hearty laugh. He's delightful to be around. As our director of coaching,

Jeffrey is well-versed in all our problem-solving tools. This came in handy when a young man he knows (I'll call him Greg) encountered some problems. Jeffrey knew right where to start.

Greg had long dreamed of going to culinary school, so it was a big deal when, upon graduation from high school, he was accepted to ICC, the International Culinary Center in New York City. His parents coughed up tens of thousands of dollars for the young man to turn his dream into reality; but as we've seen, such destination-minded thinking often leaves us longing for more.

Greg arrived in New York and registered for classes, but he soon realized he had made a mistake. He missed the opportunity to take one class altogether and had to drop a second class because he hadn't taken the prerequisite yet. When his first-year schedule was found lacking by the school's administrators, they issued him his first "ding."

Soon thereafter, he was caught drinking in the dorm—his second ding.

What he didn't know but was about to find out the hard way was that at a highly selective school like ICC, it's two dings and you're out. Greg was expelled from the program of his dreams, and the fees he had paid were not refundable. He was furious. His parents were furious. Now what was he supposed to do?

Grudgingly, he packed up his dorm room, headed back to his parents' house, and got a job waiting tables.

If he couldn't attend culinary school, at least he could do something in the food-service industry. Before long, however, living at home became too much to bear, and he decided to move out of his parents' house. He had recently started dating a young woman, and she agreed to let him move in with her.

Jeffrey said that this is where things really began to careen downhill.

"Greg quit his job at the restaurant because he didn't think he was making enough money. But at least it was a job. At least it was a paycheck. He had nowhere else to go!"

He had been paying rent to his girlfriend, so when the paychecks stopped coming in, she kicked him out.

"Eventually, I had trouble reaching him," Jeffrey said, "and then I found out why. His girlfriend had bought his phone for him—and she kept it for herself when they broke up."

So now Greg had no culinary-school degree, no job, no place to live, and no phone. Things were not looking good.

It would have been easy for Jeffrey to leave this kid to find his own way; but knowing that so much of unlocking our own potential involves helping others unlock theirs . . . , Jeffrey ran toward Greg instead of running away.

"His current state was obvious to both of us," Jeffrey said. "He was hanging out with the wrong crowd, blowing his time and money on stuff that could wreck his life, and believing things about himself that were complete and utter lies. We both agreed on the current state.

"The future state? That was tougher to pin down. I could see a future for this kid that he couldn't yet see for himself. All he saw was further struggle, further disappointment, further hopelessness, further pain. But I knew he was talented. I knew he had gifts. I knew he could build a valuable life for himself. I knew he could win. As far as I was concerned, my role was to bring into view the future state that I knew for sure could be his."

Jeffrey began having weekly conversations with Greg (who, fortunately, had bought a new phone), during which he prompted the young man to articulate his desired future state.

"I simply kept asking questions," Jeffrey said, which by now you know I think is a pretty fantastic place to start.

Jeffrey would ask him, "The dynamics you're facing—are they what you hoped would be true of you at this stage in your life?"

Greg would moan and say, "No."

"What dynamics would you like to be true for you, then?"

Greg didn't have an immediate answer for that.

When new drama entered the equation, Jeffrey asked Greg, "How's that working for you?"

When Greg's friends would drag him away from becoming the man he said he wanted to be, Jeffrey would ask, "What types of friends do you want to attract, and what are the implications of that for the person you want to become?"

It took a long time, but eventually Greg went from borrowing Jeffrey's beliefs about his future to buying into those beliefs himself.

"We're still hard at work," Jeffrey recently told me. "And we will be for quite some time. But I'm convinced that as Greg and I keep speaking aloud his desired future state and he assumes the task of becoming the kind of person for whom that future state is a reality, he'll get there."

I believe Jeffrey is right. Regardless of what a person—any person—has or hasn't done, simply planting his or her feet on the path begins to unlock potential.

Find Your Way, PAGES 173–176

1. *Seeing Jeffrey's intervention in Greg's life through the lens of the Leadership Framework, how would you put words to each of the following four categories?*

   a. *The goal and strategy Jeffrey had in mind:*

   ____

   ____

   ____

   b. *The supporting steps Jeffrey took:*

   (1) ______________________________

   (2) ______________________________

(3) ____________________

(4) ____________________

(5) ____________________

(6) ____________________

c. *The steps Jeffrey chose to track:*

(1) ____________________

(2) ____________________

(3) ____________________

(4) ____________________

(5) ____________________

(6) ____________________

d. *The shared expectations that Jeffrey fostered:*

____

____

____

2. *If you were in Jeffrey's shoes, how would you rate the progress of this project? What might still need to happen, for both you (Jeffrey) and Greg to call the experience a success someday? Note your thoughts on the lines that follow before sharing your thoughts with the group.*

____

____

____

3. *Now, it's time to see how the Leadership Framework can work for you. In the first column of the following grid, note several problems that are plaguing you today. Don't overanalyze this first step; just identify the problems.*

   After you've completed an initial brain dump, fill in the second column, describing the impact of these problems on your daily quality of life.

   Now fill in the third column, identifying who, besides you, has a vested interest in solving each problem. After completing the grid, move on to question 4.

CURRENT PROBLEMS I SEE

THE PROBLEM	THE IMPACT THIS PROBLEM IS HAVING ON MY LIFE	OTHERS WHO ARE AFFECTED BY THIS PROBLEM

4. *From the list you crafted for the previous chart (and considering the level of impact for each entry), select one problem to use in working through the Leadership Framework. Write the name of the problem in the center box, and then work clockwise from the top:*

    - *For Goal and Strategy, fill in the desired solution to the problem you have chosen.*
    - *For Supporting Steps, note as many steps as you can that relate to the achievement of the stated goal.*
    - *For Tracking Steps, identify the things you plan to measure to ensure that you stay on track toward goal-achievement.*
    - *For Shared Expectations, record descriptors of the type of environment that will be most conducive to attaining the goal in a life-enhancing and upright manner.*

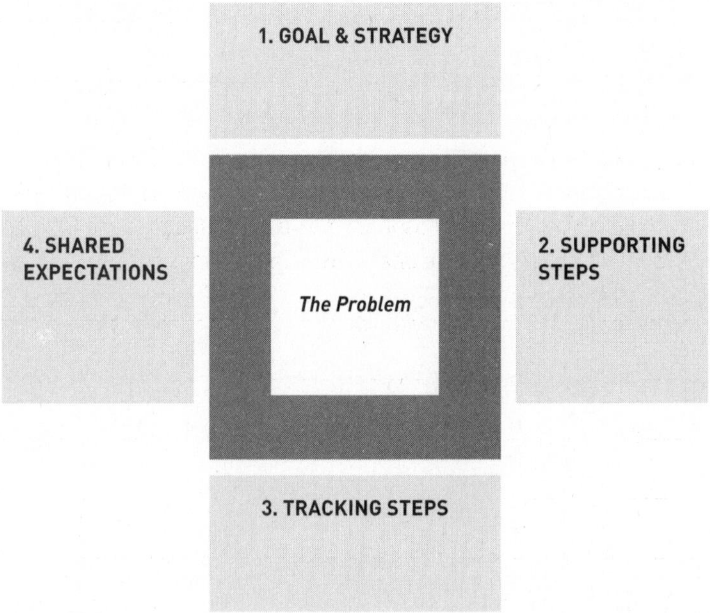

> You really can learn to view problems as opportunities. You really can choose the practices that will help you thrive. You really can live from your fullest potential. You really can help others do the same.
>
> CARLY FIORINA

5. *Now that your initial Leadership Framework is fleshed out, if you're comfortable doing so, share both the nature of the problem and the contents of one of the four categories with your group.*

   Why did you select this problem to work on? What is the reality you hope to see come to fruition through your problem-solving efforts?

___

___

___

6. *Look back at the contents of all four categories of your Leadership Framework. Record your observations as you view the problem through this lens, including things that you didn't see before. Then share one or two observations with the group.*

___

___

___

___

___

___

7. *As you address your chosen problem in such a pragmatic fashion, what is the prevailing emotion you experience?*

   - ☐ *Enthusiasm: "I can actually see a way out of this thing."*
   - ☐ *Curiosity: "I'm definitely eager to see how this all pans out."*
   - ☐ *Skepticism: "I'm not sold, but I'll give it a try."*
   - ☐ *Something else?* ______________________________

Flattening the Wave

The reason for asking about your emotions is this: As you read in chapter 10 of *Find Your Way*, there is an interesting emotional dynamic that unfolds in the life of problem solvers, involving a certain flattening-out of the wild up-and-down swings they previously knew. To begin to personalize this concept, consider the graphic below. Which of the sine waves depicted best reflects your typical emotional approach to life? Is it a "rhythmic wave," where ups and downs fall into a slow, predictable steadiness? Is it an "intermediate wave" that finds you ramping up and sinking down several times a day? Or is it an "erratic wave," which can rapidly bury the people around you, either with your effusiveness or with your despair?

1. *Pick your most typical wave from the five below, explaining to the group your rationale for the choice you made.*

MY TYPICAL EMOTIONAL TENOR

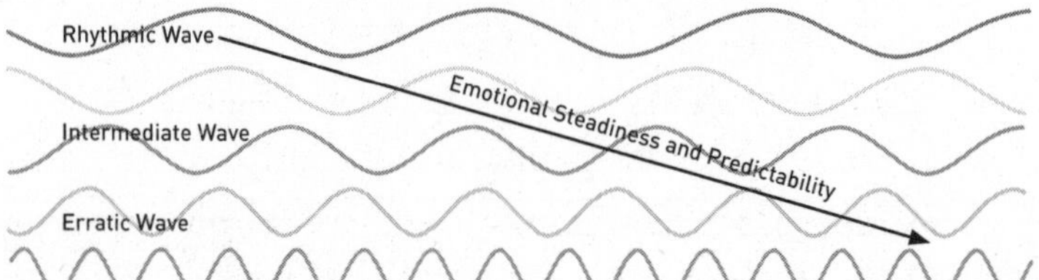

2. *If your closest friends and loved ones were asked about your emotional sine wave, what would they say?*

____

____

____

3. *How satisfied are you with your current emotional wave? What would you change about it, if anything at all?*

____

____

____

> As I've learned to run *toward* problems instead of running away from them, and as I keep trying to always choose the best version of myself over all other forms, fear has had far less sway over my decision-making. It occupies less and less of my brain.
>
> CARLY FIORINA

4. *In* Find Your Way, *Carly writes,*

    In truth, there are very few actual *crises* and very few *best-ever* experiences. Consequently, so much of the energy we expend is a colossal waste. . . .

    I bring this up because I've noticed that, as I practice following the path, there is a steadiness, a sureness, in my step. No longer do I feel subjected to the wild swings of cultural enthusiasm: We're outraged! We're elated! We're fuming! We're rejoicing! We're incredulous! We're euphoric! We're irate!

Find Your Way, PAGES 212–213

Do you agree or disagree with this sentiment about wasted energy? Why?

A Positive Contribution, Today and Every Day

If you're like most people, when you get to the end of the day you evaluate your success according to the tasks you were able to complete, by the number of items you were able to check off on your to-do list. The flaw in this way of thinking, of course, is that all tasks are not created equal. How can you know which items yielded the most good and which were inconsequential in the end?

Throughout the coming week, take the risk of approaching your days in a totally different manner, basing the assessed value of the hours you spend not on the tasks you complete, but rather on the *positive contributions* you make. Read on for further details.

Now Go (and Grow)

Before dismissing your gathering, ask each member of the group how he or she plans to implement the following action step.

View your day in a whole new way. For the next week, spend a few minutes at the end of each day assessing not the meetings you attended, the phone calls you returned, the chores you completed, or the errands you ran, but rather the positive contributions you made. Ask yourself:

- Where did I exhibit courage?
- When did I stand up for what I believe?
- In what ways did I invite others to shoulder the load with me?
- How did I see creative possibilities behind the problems I faced?

Progress begets progress. As you log the positive contributions you make, you will be inspired to make further positive contributions during the course of the week.

Today you will become more fearful or more courageous. The choice is yours.

Today you will become more scattered or more integrated. The choice is yours.

Today you will become more uncooperative with others or more cooperative. The choice is yours.

Today you will become more of a pessimist or more of an optimist. The choice is yours.

You will expand your knowledge, or not.

You will increase your circle, or not.

You will act from compassion, or not.

You will wait patiently for life, or not.

You will challenge your own prejudices, or not.

You will practice gratitude, or not.

You will help others, or not.

You will let others speak first, or not.

You will ask for help, or not.

You will encourage others, or not.

CARLY FIORINA

Looking for More?

To dive deeper into the concepts presented in session 3, complete the following section on your own.

In this "Looking for More?" section, you will dig deeper on an extended excerpt from *Find Your Way*, engage with a few evaluative and introspective exercises, and experiment with applying the core concepts to your life.

The Excerpt

In chapter 10 of *Find Your Way*, Carly offers a prime example of allowing perilous news to serve as problem-solving fuel.

> In May 2008, a friend of mine, then–secretary of state Condoleezza Rice, asked me to create an empowerment fund for women in countries where they are most oppressed. We both recognized the vast opportunities she and I have been given in America, and we were compelled to be good stewards of the lessons we had learned and the resources we had acquired along the way.
>
> Condi grew up in the segregated South, the only child of a teacher and a preacher. We each had found our way through diligent effort and a bit of luck. After all, we came of age at a time when this country was finding its conscience regarding the treatment of women; she and I were grateful for that favored spot.
>
> More immediately, though, we were compelled by a truly tragic turn of events.

Two days after Christmas in 2007, the first woman ever to head a democratic government in a Muslim-majority nation, Benazir Bhutto of Pakistan, was assassinated. She had served as prime minister twice—from 1988 to 1990 and again from 1993 to 1996. Though many viewed her as a controversial figure, she was extremely instrumental in championing democracy and women's rights in that part of the world.

On the day of her death, Ms. Bhutto had been campaigning ahead of her country's January elections. Following a political rally in Rawalpindi, Pakistan, shots were fired at her and her associates. By six o'clock that evening, she had died. We were determined not to let her death be in vain.

We lost no time gathering groups of employees of the US Agency for International Development (USAID) and the US Department of State for discussion. What bubbled to the surface was a mutual desire for justice, opportunity, and leadership on behalf of women around the world. We began mapping out strategies fairly quickly: vocational training, microlending, awareness-building regarding women's basic rights worldwide, and how to advocate for the liberty they deserved—many of the same things Benazir Bhutto had stood for. How we hoped she would have been proud.

There were lots of great organizations doing good work. I believed many of the best were local, focused on their communities, but they were also so small they weren't getting the attention and the funding they needed. So we decided to lift them up.

On the administrative side, we decided to make this a joint effort, bringing together ten partners from the private sector and both the State Department and USAID from the public sector. In terms of the recipients of the grants we would issue, organizations would simply submit applications that detailed the thrust of their cause.

Shortly after Condi and I confirmed the details of our plan, she delivered a formal statement in Washington, DC:

> In an age where women are climbing to new heights, we must pause for a moment and direct our concerns toward those who have been left behind. . . .
>
> Across this globe, we see signs of women standing up for freedom, standing up for justice and demanding opportunity. And I am proud of the work the United States is doing to support them. I am equally proud of our corporate partners for their initiative to empower, educate, and inspire women across the globe. We know that it is only by working together that we can ultimately effect change for women around the world.

As is always the case, things took longer to move ahead than we hoped, and for the first full year following our official announcement, we gave away not a single dollar. But we did raise our first round of funding, and at last grants were ready to be made. I beamed when I saw the headline on an advance release from USAID's office in early June 2009: "'One Woman Initiative' Announces First Grants to Women's Organizations in Five Nations."

The article began,

> The One Woman Initiative, a one-year-old public/private initiative to empower women in countries with significant Muslim populations, today announced its first grants, totaling more than $500,000 to five grassroots organizations in Azerbaijan, Egypt, India, Pakistan, and the Philippines. The OWI grants are being made to locally focused organizations with results-oriented programs providing women access to legal rights, political participation, and economic development.

I lingered over the details of those first five grants, imagining in my mind's eye the good they would do. When one woman—just one woman—is empowered, the world benefits. When that woman is granted access to information and training, to resources and opportunities, to advocacy and freedom and care, she can raise up her entire family, and on occasion, her community at large. To embolden ten women or one hundred women or one thousand women—as these first five grants would do—wasn't a matter of addition but of exponential effect. When entire swaths of the population in various villages and regions are given access to broad-based support, and when they are invited to participate in local workplaces, and when they are allowed to offer their expertise, opinions, and strength—well, in that scenario, the ensuing effect can be huge.

As you think of all you've read in this book, and as you reflect on your own life and your opportunities for impact, perhaps you feel small and inadequate just as often as you feel powerful and strong. Whenever you feel small, think of a pebble tossed into a still pond. The tiny pebble enters the water with barely a splash, but from there it sends ripples far and wide. Seemingly inconsequential agents can catalyze significant change. If just one person discovers that he or she has power; if just one person is shown his or her vast gifts; if just one person is taught how to stand firm and speak; if just one person learns how to dream, then ripples will begin to move across the world.

Knowing is not enough; we must apply.
Willing is not enough; we must do.

JOHANN WOLFGANG VON GOETHE

Find Your Way, pages 220–224

The Evaluation

Knowing what you now know about problem solving (including what keeps people from engaging in it), what other options could Carly have pursued besides jumping into the fray, rallying a like-minded friend, and helping out?

1. ______________________________
2. ______________________________
3. ______________________________
4. ______________________________
5. ______________________________

Based on what you know of the story, what factors made Carly and Condi's stated goal doable?

____

____

____

____

____

____

Revisiting the story, what supporting steps do you find in the women's plan?

1. ______________________________
2. ______________________________

3. ______________________________

4. ______________________________

5. ______________________________

6. ______________________________

What wisdom can be gleaned from taking in other problem-solvers' goals and strategies, supporting steps, and tracking steps? Note your thoughts in the space below before moving on.

____

____

____

The Experiment

A certain degree of peril surrounds us every moment of every day, and yet it is still entirely possible to have hope in this world. Our hope comes from knowing that the power in us is greater than the power that is in the world. Since the beginning of time, God has invited us mere mortals into the cooperative adventure of a lifetime, to join him in restoring what is broken, in and around us, to something beautiful, functional, pure.

The challenge this week is this: When you are confronted with *certain peril*, use it as fuel for problem solving instead. Take a step back from the incendiary situation and ask yourself, "What's possible here?"

You may not be able to thwart the spewing of vitriol

across all social-media platforms, but for your part, you can offer life-giving, compassionate posts.

You may not be able to solve urban gang violence across the nation, but you can engage with a young person who may be hanging with the (very) wrong crowd and offer him or her your genuine interest and a genuine smile.

You may not be able to remedy global poverty, but you can choose to live on less than your full income so that there's something left over to give away.

Perilous times can provide the ripest of ripe opportunities for problem solvers to rise up, link arms, and do what they do best. And let's be honest: What else are you going to do with your one (and only) wild and precious life?

> If just one person is shown his or her vast gifts; if just one person is taught how to stand firm and speak; if just one person learns how to dream, then ripples will begin to move across the world.
>
> CARLY FIORINA

ABOUT THE AUTHORS

CARLY FIORINA is the former Chairman and CEO of Hewlett-Packard. Carly is a true leader and a seasoned problem-solver. Her mission is to inspire, equip, and connect individuals and teams to seize opportunities, face challenges, and accelerate impact in their communities and organizations. Through Carly Fiorina Enterprises and Unlocking Potential Foundation, Carly and her team strengthen the problem-solving and leadership capacity across America. She is a sought-after speaker and adviser who wants to see people and organizations achieve their highest potential.

ASHLEY WIERSMA is a freelance writer of Christian-living and spiritual-memoir books and small-group curricula. She and her family live in the foothills of Colorado.